# Pretty Hats to Knit

*20 Step-by-step Knitting Patterns*

Copyright © 2023

All rights reserved.

**DEDICATION**

The author and publisher have provided this e-book to you for your personal use only. You may not make this e-book publicly available in any way. Copyright infringement is against the law. If you believe the copy of this e-book you are reading infringes on the author's copyright, please notify the publisher at: https://us.macmillan.com/piracy

# Contents

Bernat Basic Knit Ribbed Hat .................................................. 1

Caron Knit Hat On The Go ...................................................... 4

Caron Fading Shades Knit Hat ............................................... 10

Highligher Lines Knit Hat ....................................................... 14

Bernat Winter Weekend Hat .................................................. 19

Soft and Cozy Knit Hat .......................................................... 23

Game Day Knit Hat ............................................................... 28

Teddy Love Hat ..................................................................... 33

Rainbow Hat .......................................................................... 40

Caron Knit Rib Hat ................................................................ 48

Caron Brioche Cables Knit Hat ............................................. 52

Caron Nordic Flake Hat ........................................................ 62

Caron Medallion Knit Hat ..................................................... 67

Caron Inside Out Knit Beanie ............................................... 74

## Pretty Hats to Knit

**Caron Lumberjack Beanie** .......................................... 79

**Patons Bright Stripes Beanie** ...................................... 83

**Red Heart Ribbed Knit Beanie** .................................. 87

**Patons Breezy Knit Beret** ...........................................91

**Red Heart Buttoned Beret** ......................................... 95

**Red Heart Cabled Chapeau** ..................................... 101

Pretty Hats to Knit

# Bernat Basic Knit Ribbed Hat

**SKILL LEVEL:** Easy

**MATERIALS**

Bernat® Softee® Chunky™ (14 oz/400 g; 431 yds/394 m)

Sizes 2/4 yrs (6/10 yrs – Adult)

# Pretty Hats to Knit

Natural (30008) or Gray Ragg (30047) or Gray Heather (30046) or Teal (30203) or True Gray (30044): 1 (1-1) ball

Note: 1 ball will make 4 (3-3) Hats.

Size U.S. 10½ (6.5 mm) knitting needles or size needed to obtain gauge.

## ABBREVIATIONS

Approx = Approximately

Beg = Beginning

K = Knit

K2tog = Knit next 2 stitches together

P = Purl

P2(3)tog = Purl next 2(3) stitches together

Pat = Pattern

Rem = Remaining

Rep = Repeat

RS = Right side

St(s) = Stitch(es)

# Pretty Hats to Knit

**SIZES:** To fit head sizes

Child 2/4 years: 19" [48 cm] circumference

Child 6/10 years: 20" [51 cm] circumference

Adult: 21-22" [53.5-56 cm] circumference

**GAUGE:** 12 sts and 16 rows = 4" [10 cm] in stocking st.

## INSTRUCTIONS

The instructions are written for smallest size. If changes are necessary for larger size(s) the instructions will be written thus ( ). When only one number is given, it applies to all sizes.

Cast on 55 (59-63) sts.

1st row: *K2. P2. Rep from * to last 3 sts. K2. P1.

Rep last row for Mistake Rib Pat for 7 (8½-9½)" [18 (21.5-24) cm].

*Shape top:* 1st row: (RS). *K1. P3tog. Rep from * to last 3 sts. K1. P2tog. 28 (30-32) sts.

2nd to 6th rows: *K1. P1. Rep from * to end of row.

7th row: (RS). K1. *K2tog. Rep from * to last st. P1. 15 (16-17) sts. Break yarn leaving a long end. Draw end tightly through rem sts and fasten securely. Sew center back seam. Turn back cuff as shown.

Pompom: Wind yarn around 3 (4-4) fingers approx 70 (80-80) times. Remove from fingers and tie tightly in center. Cut through each side of loops. Trim to a smooth round shape, approx 3 (4-4)" [7.5 (10-10) cm] diameter. Sew to top of Hat.

# Caron Knit Hat On The Go

**Version 1**

**Version 2**

**SKILL LEVEL:** Easy

**MATERIALS**

Caron® Colorama™ O'Go™ (6.4 oz/180 g; 228 yds/208 m) Baja (68013) 1 O'Go (will make 2 Hats)

Size U.S. 10½ (6.5 mm) circular knitting needle 16" [40.5 cm] long. Setof 4 size U.S. 10½ (6.5 mm) double-pointed knitting needles or size needed to obtain gauge. Yarn needle.

## ABBREVIATIONS

Beg = Beginning

K = Knit

K2tog = Knit next 2 stitches together

P = Purl

Pat = Pattern

Rem = Remaining

Rep = Repeat

Rnd(s) = Round(s)

RS = Right side

Sl1Pwyib = Slip next stitch purlwise with yarn in back of work

Ssk = Slip next 2 stitches knitwise one at a time. Pass them back onto lefthand needle, then knit through back loops together

St(s) = Stitch(es)

**SIZE:** One size to fit Adult.

**GAUGE:** 12 sts and 17 rows = 4" [10 cm] in stocking st.

## INSTRUCTIONS

### *Notes:*

• To begin working with the O'Go format, carefully cut plastic tie where the ends of the O'Go meet.

• Pull tie to remove

• For Version 1, colors can be easily separated by gently pulling apart and cutting at the color transition. Each color is ready to use. Follow color guide shown in Materials section for each O'Go (Contrast A, B, C, D, E). You may find it helpful to place each color section in its own resealable (zip lock) bag and label each bag A, B, C, D, E.

## VERSION 1

Note: To make both Hats from 1 O'Go, knit Version 1 first, then use leftover yarn to knit Version 2.

Change to set of four doublepointed needles after decreases when necessary to accommodate all sts.

With circular needle and B, cast on 64 sts. Join in rnd.

# Pretty Hats to Knit

1st and 2nd rnds: *K1. P1. Rep from * around. Join E.

With E, rep last rnd of (K1. P1) ribbing until work from beg measures 4" [10 cm]. Join A.

With A, rep last rnd of (K1. P1) ribbing until work from beg measures 5" [12.5 cm].

Proceed in pat as follows:

1st rnd: With A, *K3. K1 – wrapping yarn twice around needle. Rep from * around.

2nd rnd: *K3. Sl1Pwyib, dropping extra loop. Rep from * around.

3rd and 4th rnds: *K3. Sl1Pwyib. Rep from * around.

Last 4 rnds form pat.

Keeping cont of pat, with A, work 6 rows.

With B, work 2 rows.

With C, work 10 rows.

With B, work 2 rows.

**Shape top:** 1st rnd: With D, *K2tog. K1. K1 wrapping yarn twice around needle. Rep from * around. 48 sts.

2nd rnd: *K2. Sl1Pwyib, dropping extra loop. Rep from * around.

3rd and 4th rnds: *K2. Sl1Pwyib. Rep from * around.

5th rnd: *K2tog. K1 wrapping yarn twice around needle. Rep from * around. 32 sts.

6th rnd: *K1. Sl1Pwyib, dropping extra loop. Rep from * around.

7th and 8th rnds: *K1. Sl1Pwyib. Rep from * around.

9th rnd: (K2tog) 16 times. 16 sts. Break yarn, leaving long end. Thread end through rem sts. Pull tightly. Fasten securely.

***Pompom:*** Wind B around 4 fingers 80 times. Tie tightly in the middle and leave a long end for attaching to Hat. Cut loops at both ends and trim to smooth round shape. Sew securely to top of Hat. Fold ribbing 3" [7.5 cm] to RS for brim.

## VERSION 2

Note: Use leftover shades from Version 1 in any order.

With circular needle, cast on 64 sts. Join in rnd.

1st rnd: *K1. P1. Rep from * around.

Rep last rnd of (K1. P1) ribbing for 5" [12.5 cm].

Proceed in pat as follows:

# Pretty Hats to Knit

1st rnd: *K3. K1 - wrapping yarn twice around needle. Rep from * around.

2nd rnd: *K3. Sl1Pwyib, dropping extra loop. Rep from * around.

3rd and 4th rnds: *K3. Sl1Pwyib. Rep from * around.

Rep last 4 rnds of pat until work from beg measures 9" [23 cm].

**Shape top:** 1st rnd: *K2tog. K1. K1 wrapping yarn twice around needle. Rep from * around. 48 sts.

2nd rnd: *K2. Sl1Pwyib, dropping extra loop. Rep from * around.

3rd and 4th rnds: *K2. Sl1Pwyib. Rep from * around.

5th rnd: *K2tog. K1 wrapping yarn twice around needle. Rep from * around. 32 sts.

6th rnd: *K1. Sl1Pwyib, dropping extra loop. Rep from * around.

7th and 8th rnds: *K1. Sl1Pwyib. Rep from * around.

9th rnd: (K2tog) 16 times. 16 sts. Break yarn, leaving long end. Thread end through rem sts. Pull tightly. Fasten securely.

**Pompom:** Work as Pompom in Version 1

# Caron Fading Shades Knit Hat

**SKILL LEVEL:** Easy

**MATERIALS**

Caron® Colorama™ O'Go™ (6.4 oz/180 g; 228 yds/208 m): Lippy (68004) or Blue Mustang (68015) 1 O'Go

Set of 4 sizes U.S. 9 (5.5 mm) and U.S. 10 (6 mm) double-pointed knitting needles or size needed to obtain gauge. Stitch marker.

Yarn needle.

**ABBREVIATIONS**

Beg = Begin(ning)

K = Knit

K2tog = Knit next 2 stitches together

P = Purl

Rem = Remain(ing)(s)

Rep = Repeat

Rnd(s) = Round(s)

St(s) = Stitch(es)

Tog = Together

**SIZE:** One size to fit Adult.

**GAUGE:** 13 sts and 18 rows = 4" [10 cm] in stocking st.

## INSTRUCTIONS

Notes:

• To begin working with the O'Go format, carefully cut plastic tie here the ends of the O'Go meet.

• Pull tie to remove.

• For this pattern, separate colors by gently pulling apart and cutting at the color transition. Each color is ready to use.

# Pretty Hats to Knit

- Designate each color A, B, C, D, E as indicated in Materials.

## HAT

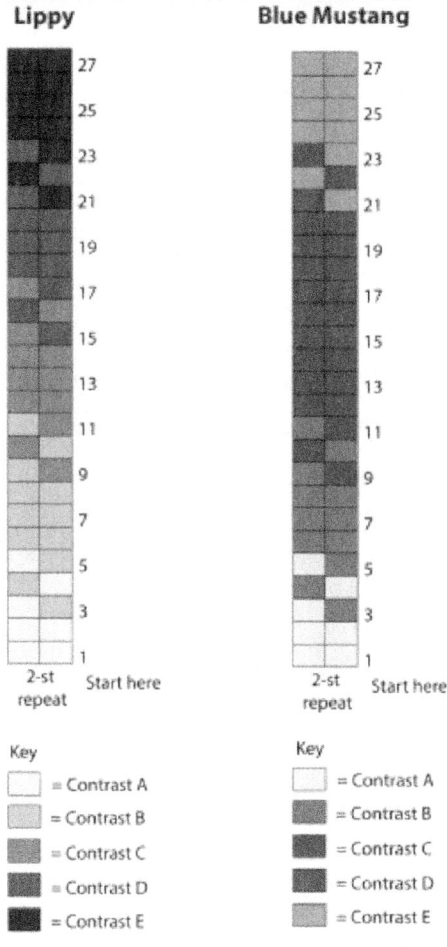

With smaller set of needles and A, cast on 68 sts. Divide sts on 3 needles (24 sts on first 2 needles and 20 sts on 3rd needle). Join in rnd, placing marker on first st.

# Pretty Hats to Knit

1st rnd: *K2. P2. Rep from * around.

Rep last rnd (K2. P2) ribbing for 2" [5 cm].

Change to larger set of needles and knit next rnd.

First rnd of Chart is complete.

Knit Chart to end of chart, reading rnds from right to left and noting 2-st rep will be worked 34 times.

**Shape top:** 1st rnd: With E, *K15. K2tog. Rep from * around. 64 sts.

2nd rnd: *K6. K2tog. Rep from * around. 56 sts.

3rd rnd: *K5. K2tog. Rep from * around. 48 sts.

4th rnd: *K4. K2tog. Rep from * around. 40 sts.

5th rnd: *K3. K2tog. Rep from * around. 32 sts.

6th rnd: *K2. K2tog. Rep from * around. 24 sts.

7th rnd: *K1. K2tog. Rep from * around. 16 sts.

8th rnd: (K2tog) 8 times. 8 sts. Break yarn leaving a long end. Draw end tightly through rem sts and fasten securely.

Pompom: With 1 strand each of A, B, C, D, and E held tog, wind yarn around 4 fingers 30 times. Remove from fingers and tie tightly in center. Cut through each side of loops. Trim to a smooth round shape. Sew to top of Hat.

# Highligher Lines Knit Hat

**SKILL LEVEL:** Easy

**MATERIALS**

Red Heart® Super Saver® O'Go™ (Solids: 7 oz/197 g; 364 yds/333 m; Prints: 5 oz/141 g; 236 yds/215 m)

Contrast A Newsprint (7124) 1 O'Go

Contrast B Gold (7160) 1 O'Go

Sizes U.S. 7 (4.5 mm) and U.S. 8 (5 mm) knitting needles or size needed to obtain gauge. Stitch marker. Yarn needle.

## ABBREVIATIONS

Approx = Approximately

K = Knit

K2tog = Knit next 2 stitches together

P = Purl

Pat = Pattern

Rem = Remaining

Rep = Repeat

RS = Right side

Sl1Pwyib = Slip next stitch purlwise with yarn in back of work

Sl1Pwyif = Slip next stitch purlwise with yarn in front of work

# Pretty Hats to Knit

St(s) = Stitch(es)

WS = Wrong side

**SIZE:** One size to fit Adult.

**GAUGE:** 17 sts and 28 rows = 4" [10 cm] in pat with larger needles.

## INSTRUCTIONS

Notes:

- To begin working with the O'Go format, carefully cut plastic tie where the ends of the O'Go meet.

- Pull tie to remove and start knitting.

- Work from O'Go as the colors flow – no need to separate colors.

## HAT

With B and smaller needles cast on 85 sts.

1st row: (RS). *K1. P1. Rep from * to last st. K1.

2nd row: *P1. K1. Rep from * to last st. P1.

Rep last 2 rows (K1. P1) ribbing for 3" [7.5 cm], ending on a WS row Place marker at end of last row.

Note: When working with 2 colors in a row, carry color not in use loosely across WS of work.

Change to larger needles and proceed in pat as follows:

1st row: (RS). With A, K2. *Sl1Pwyib. K3. Rep from * to last 3 sts. Sl1Pwyib. K2.

2nd row: With A, K2. *Sl1Pwyif. K3. Rep from * to last 3 sts. Sl1Pwyif. K2.

3rd row: With A, K2. *With B, K1. With A, K3. Rep from * to last 3 sts. With B, K1. With A, K2.

4th row: As 2nd row.

5th row: As 1st row.

6th row: With A, K2. *With B, P1. With A, K3. Rep from * to last 3 sts. With B, P1. With A, K2.

Rep last 6 rows for pat until Hat from marked row measures approx 6" [15 cm], ending on a 6th row of pat.

**Shape top:** 1st row: (RS). With A, K2. *Sl1Pwyib. K1. K2tog. Rep from * to last 3 sts. Sl1Pwyib. K2. 65 sts.

2nd row: With A, K2. *Sl1Pwyif. K2. Rep from * to last 3 sts. Sl1Pwyif. K2.

3rd row: With A, K2. *With B, K1. With A, K2. Rep from * to last 3 sts. With B, K1. With A, K2.

4th row: As 2nd row.

5th row: With A, K2tog. *Sl1Pwyib. K2tog. Rep from * to last 3 sts. Sl1Pwyib. K2tog. 45 sts.

6th row: With A, K1. *With B, P1. With A, K1. Rep from * to last 2 sts. With B, P1. With A, K1.

7th row: With A, K1. *Sl1Pwyib. K1. Rep from * to last 2 sts. Sl1Pwyib. K1.

8th row: With A, K1. *Sl1Pwyif. K1. Rep from * to last 2 sts. Sl1Pwyif. K1. Break A.

9th row: With B, K1. *K2tog. Rep from * end of row. 23 sts.

Break yarn leaving a long end. Thread end onto yarn needle and draw tightly through rem sts. Sew center back seam, reversing seam for cuff turnback.

Pompom: Wind B around 4 fingers 100 times. Tie tightly in the middle and leave a long end for attaching to Hat. Cut loops at both ends and trim to smooth round shape. Sew securely to top of Hat.

Pretty Hats to Knit

# Bernat Winter Weekend Hat

**SKILL LEVEL**: Intermediate

**MATERIALS**

Bernat® Super Value™ (7 oz/197 g; 426 yds/389 m)

Main Color (MC) Peony Pink (53417)

Contrast A Oatmeal (53010)

Sizes U.S. 7 (4.5 mm) and U.S. 8 (5 mm) circular knitting needles 16" [40.5 cm] long.

Set of four size U.S. 7 (5 mm) double-pointed knitting needles or size needed to obtain gauge. Stitch marker.

**ABBREVIATIONS:**

Approx = Approximate(ly)

Beg = Begin(ing)

Cont = Continue(ity)

Inc1 = Increase 1 stitch by knitting into front and back of next stitch.

K = Knit

K1tbl = Knit next stitch through back loop.

P = Purl

Rem = Remain(ing)

Rep = Repeat

Rnd(s) = Round(s)

St(s) = Stitch(es)

**SIZE:** One size to fit average woman.

# Pretty Hats to Knit

## GAUGE

18 sts and 24 rows = 4" [10 cm] in stocking st with larger needles.

## INSTRUCTIONS

With smaller needle and MC, cast on 86 sts. Join in rnd, placing marker on first st.

1st rnd: *K1tbl. P1. Rep from * around. Break MC. Join A.

With A, rep last rnd (K1tbl. P1) ribbing for 3" [7.5 cm].

Change to larger needle.

Next rnd: K3. Inc1. *K19. Inc1. Rep from * to last 3 sts. K3. 90 sts.

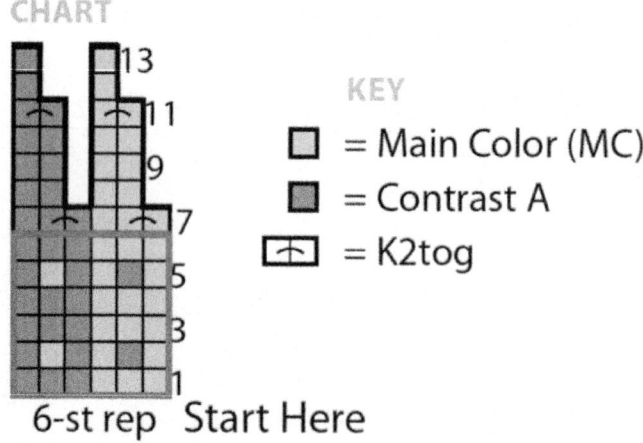

Work rnds 1 to 6 of Chart, reading rnds from right to left, noting 6 st rep will be worked 15 times.

Rep rnds 1 to 6 of Chart until Hat from beg measures approx 7½" [19 cm].

**Shape crown:** Work rnds 7 to 13 of Chart, switching to larger set of double-pointed needles when appropriate. 30 sts rem. Break yarn, leaving a long end. Draw end tightly through rem loops and fasten securely.

Pompom: Wind MC around 4 fingers approx 90 times. Tie tightly in the middle, leaving a long end for attaching to Hat. Cut loops at both ends and trim to a smooth round shape. Sew to top of Hat.

# Soft and Cozy Knit Hat

SKILL LEVEL: EASY

**MATERIALS**

RED HEART® Scrubby Smoothie ® (3.5 oz/100 g; 153 yds/140 m)

# Pretty Hats to Knit

Sizes         S M L XL

Brite Pink (9373) 1 1 1 1 ball

Sizes U.S. 6 (4 mm) and U.S. 8 (5 mm) knitting needles or size needed to obtain gauge. Yarn needle.

## ABBREVIATIONS

Alt = Alternate(ing)

Approx = Approximately

Beg = Beginning

K = Knit

K2tog = Knit next 2 stitches together

P = Purl

Pat = Pattern

Rep = Repeat

RS = Right side

WS = Wrong side

## SIZES

# Pretty Hats to Knit

Finished Head Circumference:

S 18" [46 cm]

M 20" [51 cm]

L 22" [56 cm]

XL 24" [61 cm]

**GAUGE**

18 sts and 22 rows = 4" [10 cm] with larger needles in stocking st.

**INSTRUCTIONS**

With smaller needles, cast on 82 (90-100-108) sts.

1st row: (WS). Knit.

2nd row: (RS). Knit.

3rd row: Purl.

Rep last 2 rows of stocking st until work from beg measures 2 (2-2-2½)" [5 (5-5-6) cm], ending on a knit row.

Change to larger needles and proceed as follows:

1st row: (WS). Knit.

Work 4 rows in stocking st.

Knit 4 rows (2 garter ridges).

Rep last 8 rows until work from beg measures 5 (5½-5½-6)" [12.5 (12.5-12.5-15) cm], ending on a WS row and inc 6 (6-4-4) sts evenly across last row. 88 (96-104-112)sts.

**Shape Crown**

1st row: (RS). (K6. K2tog) 11 (12-13-14) times. 77 (84-91-98) sts.

2nd and alt rows: Purl.

3rd row: (K5. K2tog) 11 (12-13-14) times. 66 (72-78-84) sts.

5th row: (K4. K2tog) 11 (12-13-14) times. 55 (60-65-70) sts.

7th row: (K3. K2tog) 11 (12-13-14) times. 44 (48-52-56) sts.

9th row: (K2. K2tog) 11 (12-13-14) times. 33 (36-39-42) sts.

11th row: (K1. K2tog) 11 (12-13-14) times. 22 (24-26-28) sts.

13th row: (K2tog) 11 (12-13-14) times. 11 (12-13-14) sts.

15th row: (K2tog) 5 (6-6-7) times. K1 (0-1-0). 6 (6-6-7) sts.

16th row: (P2tog) 3 times. P0 (0-0-1). 3 (3-3-4) sts.

17th row: K2tog. K1 (1-1-K2tog). 2 sts.

18th row: K2tog. Fasten off.

Cut yarn leaving a long end for sewing.

**FINISHING**

Sew back seam. Weave in ends.

Lower edge rolls naturally.

# Game Day Knit Hat

**SKILL LEVEL: EASY**

**MATERIALS**

RED HEART® Super Saver®: 1 skein each of 387 Soft Navy A, 311

White B, and 672 Spring Green C

Susan Bates® Knitting Needles: 4.5 mm [US 7]

Yarn needle

Susan Bates® Easy Wrap PomPom Maker or piece of heavy cardboard

GAUGE: 20 sts = 4" (10 cm), 25 rows = 4" (10 cm) in Rib Stitch. CHECK YOUR GAUGE. Use any size needles to obtain the gauge

**Finished Hat Size:** fits 20" (22") [51 (56) cm] head circumference

## ABBREVIATIONS

K = knit;

P = purl;

st(s) = stitch(es);

K2tog = knit 2 sts together;

P2tog = purl 2 sts together;

( ) = work directions in parentheses as indicated

## Knit Hat

With A, cast on 100 (112) sts.

Row 1 (Right side): (K2, P2) across.

Repeat Row 1 for pattern until piece measures approximately 5"(6") [12.5 (15) cm] from cast on edge.

Change to B, work in pattern for 4 rows.

Change to C, work in pattern for 8 rows.

Change to B, work in pattern for 4 rows.

Change to A, work in pattern until piece measure 9"(11") [ 26.7 (28) cm] from cast on edge, ending by working a wrong-side row.

**CROWN SHAPING**

Row 1 (Right side): (K2 tog, P2) across: 75(84) sts.

Row 2: (K2, P1) across.

Row 3: (K1, P2 tog) across: 50(56) sts.

Rows 4-6: (K1, P1) across.

**Size Small Only**

Row 7: P2tog, (K2 tog, P2 tog) across: 25 sts.

Row 8: K1, (P1, K1) across.

Row 9: P1, (K1, P1) across.

Row 10: K1, (P1, K1) across.

**Size Large Only**

Row 7: (P2tog, K2 tog) across: 28 sts.

Row 8: (K1, P1) across.

Row 9: (P1, K1) across.

Row 10: (K1, P1) across.

**All Sizes**

Row 11: K1, (K2tog, K1) across: 17 (19) sts.

Cut yarn leaving a 16" (40.6 cm) end.

Thread yarn needle with end and weave through remaining stitches. Draw up firm; fasten securely.

**FINISHING**

With right sides together and matching stitches, sew seam.

**Make Pompom**

With A, B, and C held together, follow our tutorial on using the Susan Bates Easy Wrap Pom-Pom Maker or follow these directions: Wrap yarn around 3½" [9 cm] piece of heavy cardboard (the more wraps, the fuller the pompom).

Gently remove wraps from cardboard. Cut a 12" (30.5 cm) length of yarn and tie it tightly around center of wraps. Do not cut the ends of this center tie. Cut ends of wraps. Fluff and trim pompom to even strands. Use ends of center tie to attach pompom to top of hat

Pretty Hats to Knit

# Teddy Love Hat

SKILL LEVEL: EASY

**MATERIALS**

RED HEART® Boutique Infinity™: 1 ball 9351 Almond

# Pretty Hats to Knit

Susan Bates® Knitting Needles: 8mm [US 11] 16" (40 cm) circular and set of 8mm [US 11] double pointed needles

Ring marker (for beginning of round), removable stitch markers (for earflap placement), yarn needle

**GAUGE:** 12 sts = 4" (10 cm); 16 rows = 4" (10 cm) in Stockinette stitch (knit on right side, purl on wrong side). CHECK YOUR GAUGE. Use any size needles to obtain the gauge.

Directions are for size Small/Medium.

Changes for size Large/X-Large are in parentheses.

Finished Circumference: 18½ (21½)" (47 (54.5) cm).

Note: Hat will stretch to fit a range of sizes.

**Notes**

1. Hat is knit, in rounds on circular needles, from the lower edge upwards. Removable markers are placed in cast-on row to indicate where earflaps will be worked later.

2. Stitches are picked up between markers to begin each earflap. Earflaps are worked back and forth in rows down to the lower point. An I-cord tie is worked beginning over the last 3 stitches of each earflap.

3. Teddy bear ears are made separately and sewn to hat.

## HAT

With circular needle, cast on 56 (64) sts.

Place a marker for beginning of round.

Taking care not to twist stitches, prepare to work in rounds.

### Place markers for Earflaps

Size Small/Medium Only: Place a removable stitch marker in the 5th, 18th, 39th, and 52nd stitch.

Size Large/X-Large Only: Place a removable stitch marker in the 6th, 21st, 44th, and 59th stitch.

### Begin Hat (Both Sizes)

Round 1 (right side): Purl.

Round 2: Knit.

Round 3: Purl.

Rounds 4–8: Knit.

Rounds 9–11: Purl.

Rounds 12–35: Repeat Rounds 4–11 three more times.

## Shape Crown

Change to double pointed needles when stitches will no longer fit comfortably on circular needle.

Round 1 (decrease round): *K6, k2tog; repeat from * around—49 (56) sts.

Round 2: Knit.

Round 3 (decrease round): *K5, k2tog; repeat from * around—42 (48) sts.

Round 4: Knit.

Round 5 (decrease round): *K4, k2tog; repeat from * around—35 (40) sts.

Rounds 6–8: Purl.

Round 9 (decrease round): *K3, k2tog; repeat from * around—28 (32) sts.

Round 10: Knit.

Round 11 (decrease round): *K2, k2tog; repeat from * around—21 (24) sts.

Round 12: Knit.

Round 13 (decrease round): K1 (0), *k2tog; repeat from * around—11 (12) sts.

Cut yarn, leaving a 12" (30.5 cm) tail. Thread tail through remaining 11 (12) sts and pull to close opening at top of hat. Weave in tail securely on wrong side

**FIRST EARFLAP**

With right side facing and circular needle, pick up and k14 (16) sts between first and 2nd earflap markers. Work back and forth in rows as if working with straight needles.

Row 1 (wrong side): Knit.

Row 2: K1, k2tog, [k3 (4), k2tog] twice, k1—11 (13) sts.

Rows 3–23: Knit.

**Shape Flap**

Row 1: K1, [k2tog, k1] 3 (4) times, k1 (0)—8 (9) sts.

Row 2: Knit.

Row 3: [K1, k2tog] 2 (3) times, k2 (0)—6 sts.

Row 4: Knit.

Row 5: [K2tog] 3 times—3 sts.

**I-Cord Tie**

With 2 double-pointed needles and working over the remaining 3 sts, *knit all the sts, do not turn work. Slide all the stitches to opposite end of needle. Carry yarn tightly across back of work, and knit all the stitches; repeat from * a total of 50 I-cord rows.

Cut yarn, leaving a long tail. Thread tail through remaining 3 sts and pull to gather end. Weave in tail securely.

**SECOND EARFLAP**

With right side facing and circular needle, pick up and k14 (16) sts between 3rd and 4th earflap markers. Work back and forth in rows as if working with straight needles.

Make same as first earflap.

**TEDDY BEAR EARS (make 2)**

With circular needle, cast on 21 sts. Work back and forth in rows as if working with straight needles.

Rows 1–3: Knit.

Row 4: *K1, k2tog; repeat from * to end of row—14 sts.

Row 5: Knit.

Row 6: *K2tog; repeat from * to end of row—7 sts.

Row 7: Knit.

Cut yarn, leaving a 16" (40.5 cm) tail. Thread tail through remaining 7 sts and pull to gather. Sew center seam to form circle shaped ears.

**FINISHING**

Sew ears to hat, placing them diagonally between Rounds 28 and 32. Weave in ends.

**ABBREVIATIONS**

k = knit; k2tog = knit next 2 sts together; st(s) = stitch(es); [ ] = work directions in brackets the number of times specified; * = repeat whatever follows the * as indicated.

Pretty Hats to Knit

# Rainbow Hat

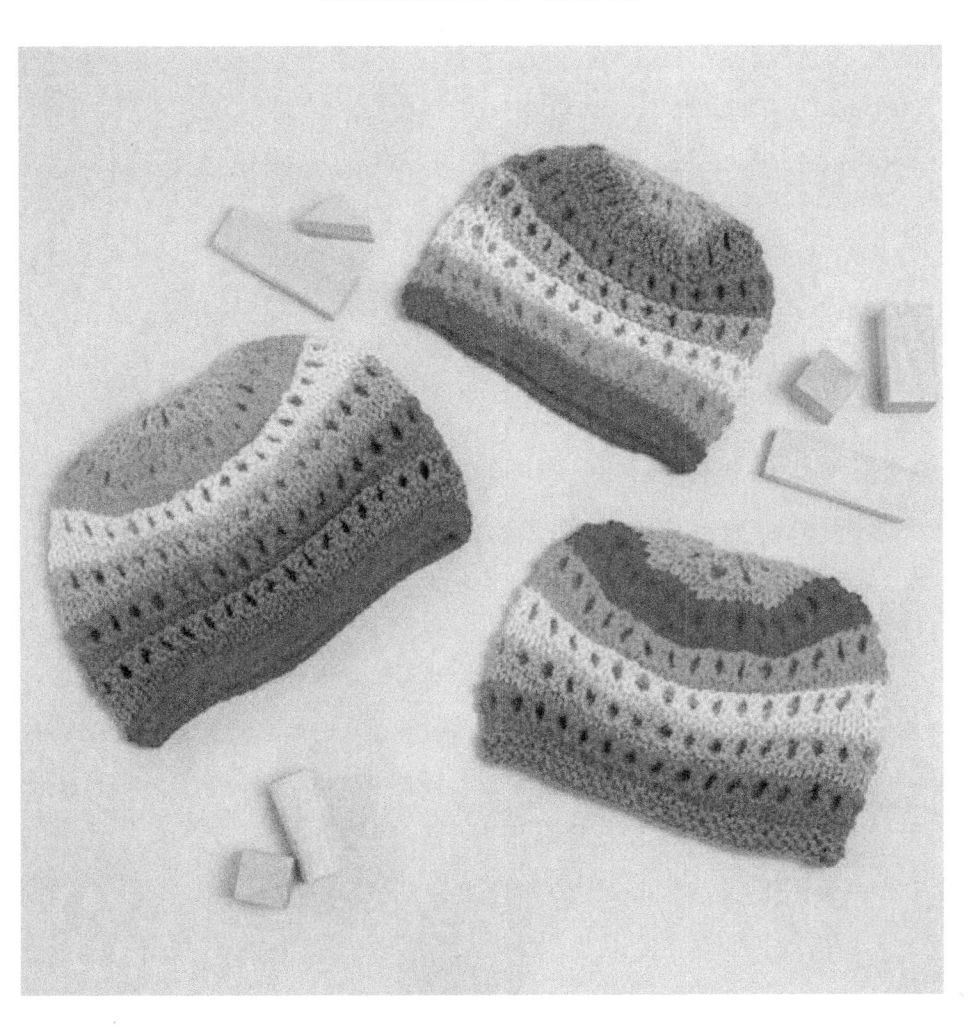

SKILL LEVEL: INTERMEDIATE

**MATERIALS**

RED HEART® Super Saver: 1 skein each of 319 Cherry Red A, 528

# Pretty Hats to Knit

Medium Purple B, 886 Blue C, 672 Spring Green D, 324 Bright Yellow E, 254 Pumpkin F, 706 Perfect Pink G

Susan Bates® Circular Knitting Needles: 6.5 mm [US 10½] 16" (40.5 cm). Susan Bates® Double-Pointed Knitting Needles: 6.5 mm [US 10½]

Stitch marker

Yarn needle

GAUGE: 14 sts = 4" (10 cm) 20 rounds = 4" (10 cm) in Stockinette Stitch. CHECK YOUR GAUGE. Use any size needles to obtain the gauge.

Directions are for size Small; changes for sizes Medium and Large are in parentheses. When only 1 number is given, it applies to all sizes.

**Finished circumference:** 16½" (18½", 20½") [42 (47, 52) cm]

**Finished height:** 7¼ (8½, 9¾)" [18.5 (21.5, 25) cm]

**NOTES**

1. Hat is worked in rounds, beginning at the lower edge.

2. Slip marker as you come to it.

3. Work begins on circular needle. When stitches no longer fit

comfortably on circular needle, change to double pointed needles.

4. To work Garter Stitch, * knit 1 round, purl one round; repeat from * for desired amount of rounds.

5. At the end of round 2 of Texture Pattern, yo needs to be worked slightly differently because it's being worked between a knit stitch (the last k2tog from round 2) and a purl stitch (the first purl stitch on round 3). Bring the yarn from the back to the front between the needles and wrap it around the right-hand needle, then bring it back to the front between the two needles to make the purl stitch.

## STITCH PATTERN

**TEXTURE PATTERN** (multiple of 2 sts)

Round 1: Purl.

Round 2: *K2tog, yo; repeat from * around.

Round 3: Purl.

## HAT STRIPE SEQUENCE

## SMALL

Cherry Red A (garter stitch edge)

Pumpkin F

# Pretty Hats to Knit

Bright Yellow E

Spring Green D

Blue C

Medium Purple B

Perfect Pink G

**MEDIUM**

Medium Purple B (garter stitch edge)

Blue C

Spring Green D

Bright Yellow E

Pumpkin F

Cherry Red A

Perfect Pink G

**LARGE**

Cherry Red A (garter stitch edge)

Medium Purple B

# Pretty Hats to Knit

Blue C

Spring Green D

Bright Yellow E

Pumpkin F

Perfect Pink G

**HAT**

With A (B, A), cast on 56 (62, 70) stitches.

Join, being careful that stitches are not twisted, and begin working in the round.

Place marker for beginning of round.

Work in Garter st and continue until piece measures 1" [2.5 cm], increasing 2 stitches in last round of Medium and Large sizes ONLY - 56 (64, 72) sts.

Change to F (C, B).

Rounds 1-2 (1-3, 1-4): Work in St st.

Rounds 3-5 (4-6, 5-7): Work in Texture pattern (3 rounds).

Repeat Rounds 1-5 (1-6, 1-7), changing colors at beginning of each repeat as noted in Hat Stripe Sequence.

Note: Read ahead as Crown shaping begins on specific round.

Continue working in pattern as established until piece measures 5½ (6¾, 8)" [14 (17, 20.5) cm] and last round worked is the round before the specific crown directions noted in Shape Crown section.

**SHAPE CROWN**

**SMALL**

(Note: Decreases begin on Round 1 of Texture pattern in B.) Dec Round 1: *P6, p2tog; repeat from * round – 49 sts.

Work Round 2 of Texture pattern.

Dec Round 2: *P5, p2tog; repeat from * around – 42 sts.

Change to G.

Dec Round 3: *K4, k2tog; repeat from * around – 35 sts.

Dec Round 4: *K3, k2tog; repeat from * around – 28 sts.

Dec Round 5: *P2, p2tog; repeat from * around – 21 sts.

Work Round 2 of Texture pattern.

Dec Round 6: *P1, p2tog; repeat from * around – 14 sts.

Dec Round 7: *K2tog; repeat from * around – 7 sts.

**MEDIUM**

(Note: Decreases begin on Round 3 of Texture pattern in A.)

Dec Round 1: *P6, p2tog; repeat from * around – 56 sts.

Change to G.

Dec Round 2: *K5, k2tog; repeat from * around – 48 sts.

Dec Round 3: *K4, k2tog; repeat from * around – 40 sts.

Dec Round 4: *K3, k2tog; repeat from * around – 32 sts.

Dec Round 5: *P2, p2tog; repeat from * around – 24 sts.

Work Round 2 of Texture pattern.

Dec Round 6: *P1, p2tog; repeat from * around – 16 sts.

Dec Round 7: *K2tog; repeat from * around – 8 sts.

**LARGE** (Note: Decreases begin on Round 1 of St st in G.)

Dec Round 1: *K6, k2tog; repeat from * around – 63 sts.

Dec Round 2: *K5, k2tog; repeat from * around – 54 sts.

Dec Round 3: *K4, k2tog; repeat from * around – 45 sts.

Dec Round 4: *K3, k2tog; repeat from * around – 36 sts.

Dec Round 5: *P2, p2tog; repeat from * around – 27 sts.

Work Round 2 of Texture pattern.

Dec Round 6: *P1, p2tog; repeat from * around – 18 sts.

Dec Round 7: *K2tog; repeat from * around – 9 sts.

## FINISHING

Cut yarn leaving a tail 8" [20.5 cm] long.

Thread tail into yarn needle and draw through remaining stitches. Pull tightly, secure and fasten off.

Weave in ends.

## ABBREVIATIONS

A, B, etc = Color A, B, etc; dec = decrease; k = knit; k2tog = knit 2 stitches together; p = purl; p2tog = purl 2 stitches together; St st = Stockinette stitch; st(s) = stitch(es); yo = yarn over; * or ** = repeat whatever follows the * or ** as indicated..

Pretty Hats to Knit

# Caron Knit Rib Hat

**SKILL LEVEL:** Intermediate

**MATERIALS**

Caron® Chunky Cakes™ (9.8 oz/280 g; 297 yds/271 m)

Blueberry Shortbread (17010) 1 ball

Size U.S. 11 (8 mm) knitting needles or size needed to obtain gauge.

## ABBREVIATIONS

Approx = Approximate(ly)

Beg = Begin(ning)

K = Knit

K1below = Knit into next stitch 1 row below, at same time slipping off stitch above

K2tog = Knit next 2 stitches together

M1 = Make 1 stitch by picking up horizontal loop lying before next stitch and knitting into back of loop

P = Purl

Pat = Pattern

Psso = Pass slipped stitch over

Rep = Repeat

Rnd(s) = Round(s)

RS = Right Side

Sl1 = Slip next stitch knitwise

# Pretty Hats to Knit

St(s) = Stitch(es)

WS = Wrong side

**SIZE:** One size to fit average Woman's head.

## GAUGE

11 sts and 14 rows = 4" [10 cm] in stocking st.

## INSTRUCTIONS

Cast on 48 sts.

1st row: (RS). *K1. P1. Rep from * to end of row.

Rep last row (K1. P1) ribbing 3 times more.

Next row: (RS). K1. *M1. K2. Rep from * to last st. M1. K1. 72 sts.

Proceed in pat as follows:

1st row: (WS). Knit.

2nd row: K1. *P1. K1below. Rep from * to last st. P1.

Rep last 2 rows for pat until work from beg measures 7" [18 cm], ending on a RS row.

***Shape Crown:*** 1st row: (WS). K3. *Sl1. K2tog. psso. K6. Rep from * to last 6 sts. Sl1. K2tog. psso. K3. 56 sts.

# Pretty Hats to Knit

2nd and alt rows: K1. *P1. K1below. Rep from * to last st. P1. (Note: When working K1below into st that has been decreased on previous row, insert needle into all sts to avoid dropped sts).

3rd row: K2. *Sl1. K2tog. psso. K4. Rep from * to last 5 sts. Sl1. K2tog. psso. K2. 40 sts.

5th row: K1. *Sl1. K2tog. psso. K2. Rep from * to last 4 sts. Sl1. K2tog. psso. K1. 24 sts.

7th row: *Sl1. K2tog. psso. Rep from * to end of row. 8 sts. Break yarn, leaving a long end. Draw through all sts tightly. Fasten securely. Sew back seam.

**Pompom:** Wind yarn around 4 fingers approx 100 times. Remove from fingers and tie tightly in center. Cut through each side of loops. Trim to smooth round shape. Sew to top of Hat

Pretty Hats to Knit

# Caron Brioche Cables Knit Hat

**SKILL LEVEL:** Intermediate

**MATERIALS**

Caron® Colorama™ O'Go™ (6.4 oz/180 g; 228 yds/208 m)

First Blush (68009) 1 O'Go

Lippy (68004) 1 O'Go

Sizes U.S. 8 [5 mm] and U.S. 10 [6 mm] circular knitting needles 16" [40.5 cm] long. Set of 4 size U.S. 8 (5 mm) double-pointed knitting needles or size needed to obtain gauge. Stitch marker. Yarn needle.

## ABBREVIATIONS

Alt = Alternate(ing)

Beg = Beginning

BrDecR = (Worked over 3 stitches)

**BRIOCHE RIGHT DECREASE**

**BrDecR** = Worked over 3 stitches (A, B, C).

1) Slip next stitch (A) knit-wise with yarn at back of work (Sl1yo).

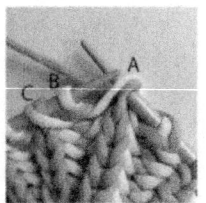

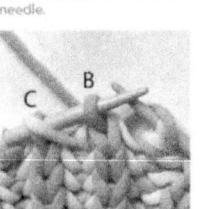

3) Knit next stitch (B).

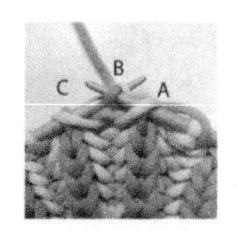

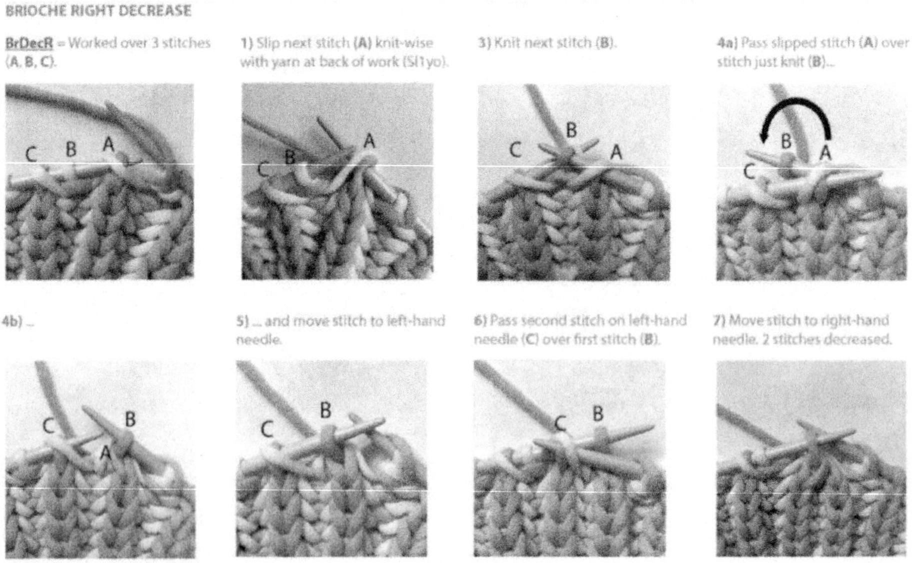

4a) Pass slipped stitch (A) over stitch just knit (B)...

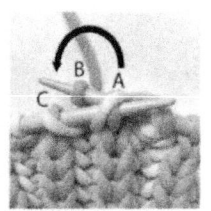

4b) ...

5) ...and move stitch to left-hand needle.

6) Pass second stitch on left-hand needle (C) over first stitch (B).

7) Move stitch to right-hand needle. 2 stitches decreased.

BrK1 = Brioche knit stitch.

# Pretty Hats to Knit

**BrK1** = Knit next stitch together with accompanying yarn over.

BrP1 = Brioche purl stitch.

**BrP1** = Purl next stitch together with accompanying yarn over.

Cont = Continue(ity)

K = Knit

K1tbl = Knit next stitch through back loop

K2tog = Knit next 2 stitches together

Pat = Pattern

Rem = Remain(ing)

Rnd(s) = Round(s)

Sl1K = Slip next st knitwise

Sl1yo

Sl1yo = Slip next stitch purl-wise with yarn in front of work, bringing yarn over needle (and over slipped stitch) to back of work. Yarn is in place to work a BrK1 stitch. If Sl1yo precedes a BrP1 stitch, bring yarn under needle to front of work to maintain yo before working BrP1 stitch.

Sl1yo before BrK1

Sl1yo before BrP1

P1tbl = Purl next stitch through back loop

St(s) = Stitch(es)

**SIZE:** One size to fit average Adult.

## GAUGES

12 sts and 32 rows = 4" [10 cm] in brioche pat on smaller needles.

13 sts and 20 rows = 4" [10 cm] in twisted rib pat on larger needles.

## INSTRUCTIONS

Notes:

- To begin working with the O'Go format, carefully cut plastic tie where the ends of the O'Go meet.

# Pretty Hats to Knit

- Pull tie to remove.

- For this pattern, colors can be easily separated by gently pulling apart and cutting at the color transition. Each color is ready to use.

- Designate each color A, B, C, D, E, F, G, H as indicated in Materials.

Note that D and E are in both First Blush and Lippy O'Gos.

- The wrap (yarn over) created by Sl1yo does not count as a separate stitch and should be treated as one stitch along with slipped stitch it accompanies.

## HAT

With A and larger circular needle, cast on 64 sts. Join in rnd, placing marker on first st.

1st to 8th rnds: *K1tbl. P1tbl. Rep from * around.

### *Stripe Pat*

Note: Stripe Pat refers to odd-numbered rnds only. All even-numbered rnds are worked in E.

With B, work 5 rnds.

With F, work 5 rnds.

With C, work 5 rnds.

With G, work 5 rnds.

With D, work 5 rnds.

With H, work 5 rnds.

These 30 rnds form Stripe Pat for odd-numbered rnds.

Change to smaller circular needle and proceed as follows in Stripe Pat

Set up Brioche Pat: 1st rnd: With B, *K1. Sl1yo. Rep from * around.

2nd rnd: With E, *Sl1yo. BrP1. Rep from * around.

First rnd of Stripe Pat is now in position.

Keeping cont of Stripe Pat, proceed in **Brioche Cable Pat** as follows (see Chart I below)

1st rnd: *BrK1. Sl1yo. BrDecR. Sl1yo. (BrK1. Sl1yo) 5 times. Rep from * around. 56 sts.

2nd rnd: *Sl1yo. BrP1. Rep from * around.

3rd rnd: *BrK1. Sl1yo. Rep from * around.

4th rnd: As 2nd rnd.

5th rnd: *BrDecR. Sl1yo. (BrK1. yo. BrK1) all in next st. Sl1yo.

(BrK1. Sl1yo) 5 times. Rep from * around.

6th rnd: *Sl1yo. BrP1. Sl1yo. P1. (Sl1yo. BrP1) 5 times. Rep from * around.

7th rnd: As 3rd rnd.

8th rnd: As 2nd rnd.

9th rnd: *BrK1. Sl1yo. (BrK1. yo. BrK1) all in next st. Sl1yo. (BrK1. Sl1yo) 5 times. Rep from * around. 64 sts.

10th rnd: As 6th rnd.

11th rnd: As 3rd rnd.

12th rnd: As 2nd rnd.

13th rnd: *(BrK1. Sl1yo) 5 times. BrDecR. Sl1yo. BrK1. Sl1yo. Rep from * around. 56 sts.

14th rnd: As 2nd rnd.

15th rnd: As 3rd rnd.

16th rnd: As 2nd rnd.

17th rnd: *(BrK1. Sl1yo) 4 times. Sl1yo. BrDecR. Sl1 yo. (BrK1. yo. BrK1) all in next st. Sl1yo. Rep from * around.

**18th rnd:** *(Sl1yo. BrP1) 5 times. Sl1yo. P1. Sl1yo. BrP1. Rep from * around.

**19th rnd:** As 3rd rnd.

**20th rnd:** As 2nd rnd.

**21st rnd:** *(BrK1. Sl1yo) 5 times. (BrK1. yo. BrK1) all in next st. Sl1yo. BrK1. Sl1yo. Rep from * around. 64 sts.

**22nd rnd:** *(Sl1yo. BrP1) 5 times. Sl1yo. P1. (Sl1yo. BrP1) twice. Rep from * around.

**23rd rnd:** As 3rd rnd.

**24th rnd:** As 2nd rnd.

These 24 rnds form Brioche Cable Pat.

Rep 1st to 22nd rnds of Brioche Cable Pat once more.

Note: Change to set of 4 smaller needles during crown shaping as necessary.

### Shape Crown: (see Chart II below)

**1st rnd:** *BrK1. Sl1yo. Rep from * around.

**2nd and alt rnds:** With E, *Sl1yo. BrP1. Rep from * around. **3rd rnd:** *BrK1. Sl1yo. BrDecR. Sl1yo. (BrK1. Sl1yo) 5 times. Rep from * around. 56 sts.

5th rnd: *BrDecR. Sl1yo. (BrK1. Sl1yo) 5 times. Rep from * around. 48 sts.

7th rnd: *BrDecR. Sl1yo. (BrK1. Sl1yo) 4 times. Rep from * around. 40 sts.

9th rnd: *(BrK1. Sl1yo) twice. BrDecR. Sl1yo. BrK1. Sl1yo. Rep from * around. 32 sts.

11th rnd: *BrK1. Sl1yo. BrDecR. Sl1yo. BrK1. Sl1yo. Rep from * around. 24 sts.

12th rnd: As 2nd rnd. Break yarn, leaving a long end. Draw end tightly through rem 24 sts and fasten securely.

Pompom: Wind A around 4 fingers approx 100 times. Remove from fingers and tie tightly in center. Cut through each side of loops. Trim to a smooth round shape. Sew pompom to top of Hat.

# Pretty Hats to Knit

## Chart I: Brioche Cable

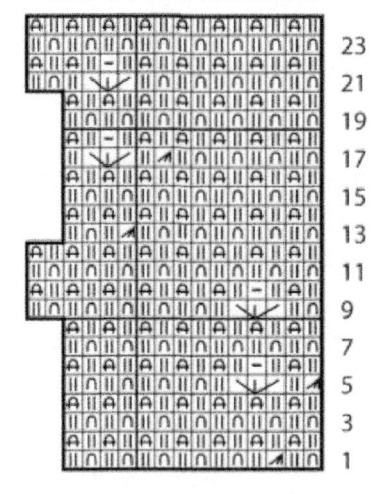

## Chart II: Crown Shaping

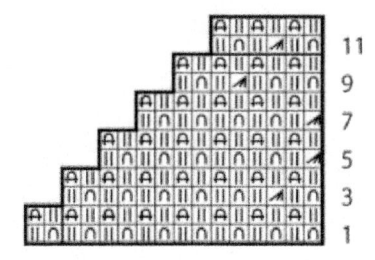

Key
- ◢ = BrDecR
- ∩ = BrK1
- ⌣ = BrK1. yo. BrK1.
- ᗅ = BrP1
- ☐ = Knit
- ⊟ = Purl
- ⊞ = Sl1yo

61

Pretty Hats to Knit

# Caron Nordic Flake Hat

**SKILL LEVEL:** Intermediate

**MATERIALS**

Caron® Simply Soft® (6 oz/170.1 g; 315 yds/288 m)

Contrast A Black (39727) 1 ball

Contrast B Off White (39702) 1 ball

Set of 4 sizes U.S. 6 (4 mm) and U.S. 7 (4.5 mm) double-pointed knitting needles or size needed to obtain gauge. 1 stitch marker.

**ABBREVIATIONS:**

Approx = Approximately

Beg = Begin(ning)

K = Knit

K2tog = Knit next 2 stitches together

M1 = Make 1 stitch by picking up horizontal loop lying before next stitch and knitting into back of loop

P = Purl

Rem = Remain(ing)

Rep = Repeat

Rnd(s) = Round(s)

St(s) = Stitch(es)

**SIZE:** One size to fit average Woman.

# Pretty Hats to Knit

## GAUGE

19 sts and 25 rows = 4" [10 cm] in stocking stitch with larger needles.

## INSTRUCTIONS

Note: When working from Charts carry color not in use loosely across WS of work but never over more than 5 sts.

When it must pass over more than 5 sts, weave it over and under the center point of sts it passes over. The colors are never twisted around one another.

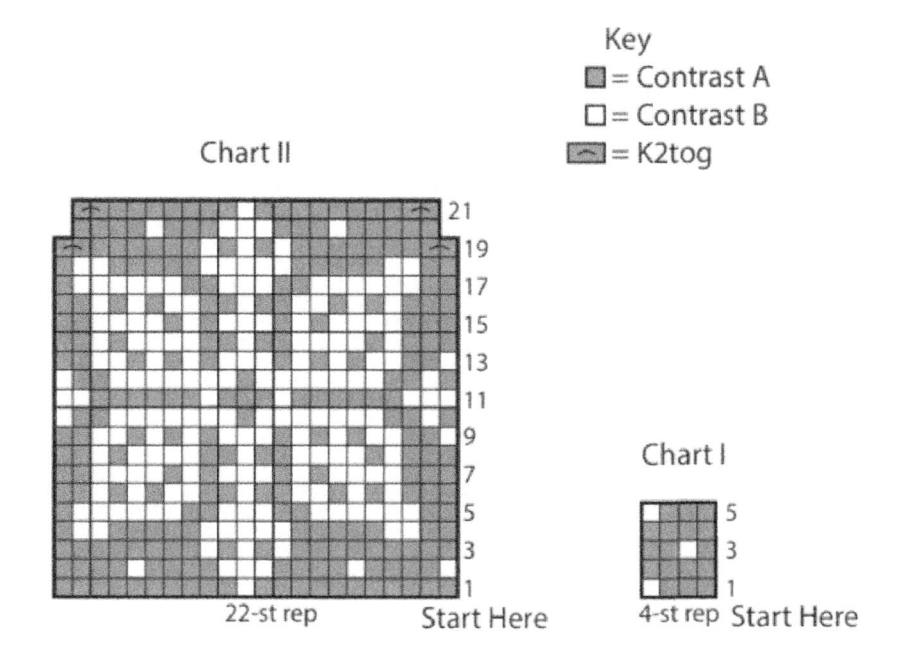

**Key**
■ = Contrast A
□ = Contrast B
◤ = K2tog

**Chart II** — 22-st rep, Start Here (rows 1–21)

**Chart I** — 4-st rep, Start Here (rows 1–5)

With A and smaller set of needles cast on 104 sts. Divide sts onto 3

## Pretty Hats to Knit

needles (36, 36, 32) sts. Join in rnd, placing a marker on first st.

1st rnd: *K2. P2. Rep from * around. Rep last rnd (K2. P2) ribbing until work from beg measures 4½" [11.5 cm].

Change to larger set of needles.

Knit 1 rnd.

Work Chart I to end of chart, noting 4-st rep will be worked 26 times

Next rnd: With A, (K16. M1. K18. M1) 3 times. K2. 110 sts.

Work Chart II to end of chart, noting 22-st rep will be worked 5 times. 90 sts rem.

**Shape crown:** 1st rnd: With A, *K3. K2tog. Rep from * around. 72 sts rem.

2nd rnd: *With B, K1. With A, K3. Rep from * around.

3rd rnd: With A, *K2. K2tog. K1. K2tog. Rep from * to last 2 sts. K2 52 sts rem.

4th rnd: *With A, K1. With B, K1. With A, K2. Rep from * around. Break B.

5th rnd: With A, *K2tog. Rep from * around. 26 sts rem.

6th rnd: Knit.

7th rnd: *K2tog. Rep from * around. 13 sts rem. Break yarn, leaving a long end. Thread end through rem 13 sts. Draw up and fasten securely.

Pompom: Wind A around 4 fingers approx 150 times. Remove from fingers and tie tightly in center. Cut through each side of loops. Trim to a smooth round shape. Sew to top of Hat.

Pretty Hats to Knit

# Caron Medallion Knit Hat

**SKILL LEVEL:** Intermediate

**MATERIALS**

Caron® Simply Soft® Speckle™ (5 oz/141 g; 235 yds/215 m)

Clorophyll (61012) 1 ball

Sizes U.S. 5 (3.75 mm) and U.S. 6 (4 mm) knitting needles or size needed to obtain gauge.

## ABBREVIATIONS

K = Knit

K2tog = Knit next 2 stitches together

P = Purl

P2sso = Pass 2 slipped stitches over

Pat = Pattern

Rem =Remaining

Rep = Repeat

RS = Right side

Ssk = Slip next 2 stitches knitwise one at a time. Pass them back onto left-hand needle, then knit through back loops together

Sl2 = Slip next 2 stitches knitwise at once as if to K2tog

St(s) = Stitch(es)

Yo = Yarn over

# Pretty Hats to Knit

**SIZE:** One size to fit Adult.

**GAUGE:** 20 sts and 26 rows = 4" [10 cm] with larger needles in stocking st.

## INSTRUCTIONS

With smaller needles, cast on 114 sts (multiple of 16 sts + 2).

See Chart:

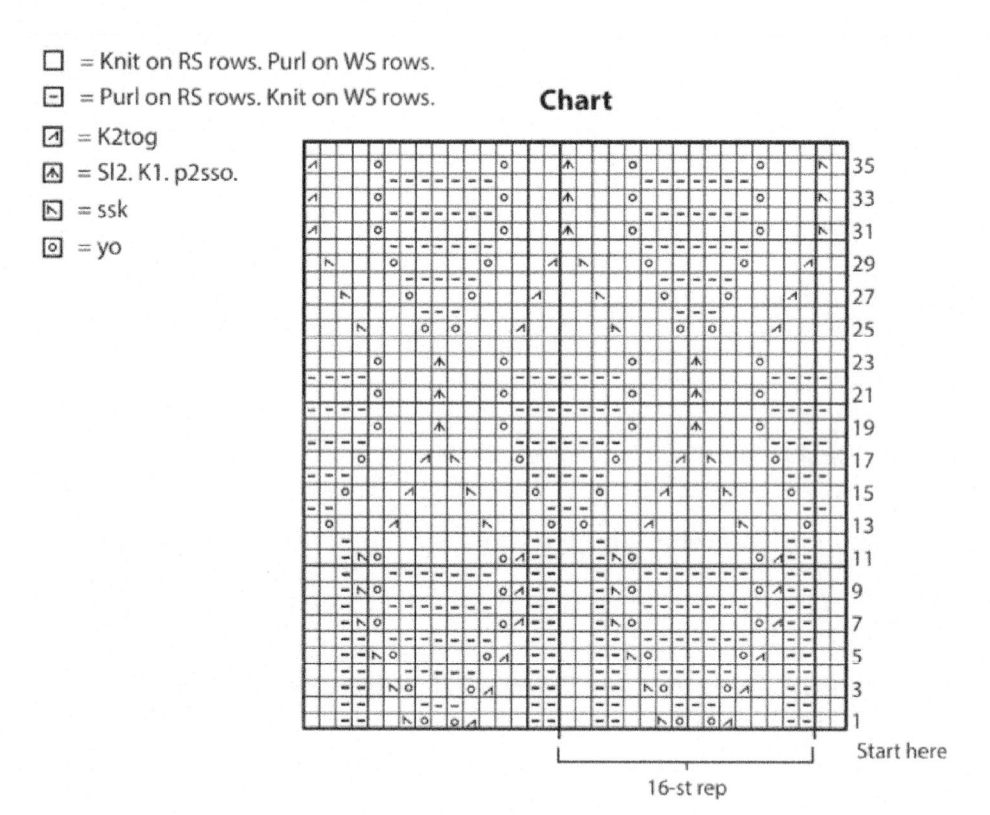

☐ = Knit on RS rows. Purl on WS rows.
⊟ = Purl on RS rows. Knit on WS rows.
◿ = K2tog
⩘ = Sl2. K1. p2sso.
◺ = ssk
◯ = yo

**Chart**

16-st rep

Start here

# Pretty Hats to Knit

1st row: (RS). K2. *P2. K2. Rep from * to end of row.

2nd row: P2. *K2. P2. Rep from * to end of row.

Rep last 2 rows of (K2. P2) ribbing 4 times more.

Change to larger needles and proceed as follows:

1st row: (RS). K2. *P2. K3. K2tog. yo. K1. yo. ssk. K2. P2. K2. Rep from * to end of row.

2nd row: *P2. K2. P3. K3. P4. K2. Rep from * to last 2 sts. P2.

3rd row: K2. *P2. K2. K2tog. yo. K3. yo. ssk. K1. P2. K2. Rep from * to end of row.

4th row: *P2. K2. P2. K5. P3. K2. Rep from * to last 2 sts. P2.

5th row: K2. *P2. K1. K2tog. yo. K5. yo. ssk. P2. K2. Rep from * to end of row.

6th row: *P2. K2. P1. K7. P2. K2. Rep from * to last 2 sts. P2.

7th row: K2. *P2. K2tog. yo. K7. yo. ssk. P1. K2. Rep from * to end of row.

8th row: *P2. K1. P2. K7. P2. K2. Rep from * to last 2 sts. P2.

9th and 10th rows: As 7th and 8th rows.

11th row: As 7th row.

12th row: *P2. K1. P11. K2. Rep from * to last 2 sts. P2.

Proceed in pat as follows:

13th row: (RS). K2. *yo. K3. ssk. K5. K2tog. K3. yo. K1. Rep from * to end of row.

14th row: *K2. P13. K1. Rep from * to last 2 sts. K1. P1.

15th row: K2. *K1. yo. K3. ssk. K3. K2tog. K3. yo. K2. Rep from * to end of row.

16th row: *K3. P11. K2. Rep from * to last 2 sts. K1. P1.

17th row: K2. *K2. yo. K3. ssk. K1. K2tog. K3. yo. K3. Rep from * to end of row.

18th row: *K4. P9. K3. Rep from * to last 2 sts. K1. P1.

19th row: K2. *K3. yo. K3. Sl2. K1. p2sso. K3. yo. K4. Rep from * to end of row.

20th to 23rd rows: As 18th and 19th rows twice.

24th row: Purl.

25th row: K2. *K2. K2tog. K3. yo. K1. yo. K3. ssk. K3. Rep from * to end of row.

## Pretty Hats to Knit

26th row: *P7. K3. P6. Rep from * to last 2 sts. P2.

27th row: K2. *K1. K2tog. (K3. yo) twice. K3. ssk. K2. Rep from * to end of row.

28th row: *P6. K5. P5. Rep from * to last 2 sts. P2.

29th row: K2. *K2tog. K3. yo. K5. yo. K3. ssk. K1. Rep from * to end of row.

30th row: *P5. K7. P4. Rep from * to last 2 sts. P2.

31st row: K1. ssk. *K3. yo. K7. yo. K3. Sl2. K1. p2sso. Rep from * to last 15 sts. K3. yo. K7. yo. K3. K2tog.

32nd to 35th rows: As 30th and 31st rows twice.

36th rows: Purl.

Rep 13th to 24th rows once more.

**Shape top:** 1st row: (RS). K2. *K2. K2tog. K7. ssk. K3. Rep from * to end of row. 100 sts.

2nd row: *P7. K1. P6. Rep from * to last 2 sts. P2.

3rd row: K2. *K1. K2tog. K7. ssk. K2. Rep from * to end of row. 86 sts.

4th row: *P5. K3. P4. Rep from * to last 2 sts. P2.

5th row: K2. *K2tog. K7. ssk. K1. Rep from * to end of row. 72 sts.

6th row: *P3. K5. P2. Rep from * to last 2 sts. P2.

7th row: K1. ssk. *K7. Sl2. K1. p2sso. Rep from * to last 9 sts. K7. K2tog. 58 sts.

8th row: *P3. P2tog. P3. Rep from * to last 2 sts. P2. 51 sts.

9th row: K1. ssk. *K4. Sl2. K1. p2sso. Rep from * to last 6 sts. K4. K2tog. 37 sts.

10th row: *P1. P2tog. P2. Rep from * to last 2 sts. P2. 30 sts.

11th row: K1. ssk. *K1. Sl2. K1. p2sso. Rep from * to last 3 sts. K1. K2tog. 16 sts. Break yarn, leaving a long end. Thread end through rem sts. Pull tightly. Fasten securely. Sew back seam.

# Caron Inside Out Knit Beanie

**SKILL LEVEL**: Easy

**MATERIALS**

Caron® Colorama™ Halo O'Go™ (8 oz/227 g; 481 yds/440 m) Bluestone Frost (28004) 1 O'Go or 236 yds/216 m

Size U.S. 10 (6 mm) circular knitting needle 16" [40.5 cm] long. Set of

4 size U.S. 10 (6 mm) double-pointed knitting needles or size needed to obtain gauge. 2 stitch markers. Yarn needle

## ABBREVIATIONS

Approx = Approximately

Beg = Begin(ning)

Cont = Continue(ity)

K = Knit

Kfb = Increase 1 stitch by knitting into front and back of next stitch

K2tog = Knit next 2 stitches together

PM = Place marker

Rem = Remaining

Rep = Repeat

Rnd(s) = Round(s)

St(s) = Stitch(es)

**SIZE:** One size to fit adult.

**GAUGE:** 15 sts and 20 rows = 4" [10 cm] in stocking st.

## INSTRUCTIONS

Notes:

• To begin working with the O'Go format, carefully cut plastic tie where the ends of the O'Go meet.

• Pull tie to remove.

• For a fuller ombre experience in this smaller project, remove approx 1/8 of yarn from both lightest and darkest ends of O'Go before beginning project to work across central shade transition (as shown in diagram below).

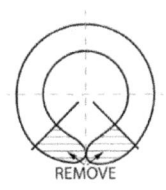

• Double thickness hat is worked in one long tube from crown to crown.

## HAT

Beg at top of crown, working from lightest end of O'Go with double pointed needles, cast on 8 sts, leaving a 12" [30.5 cm] long yarn tail for cinching crown. Join in rnd. PM for beg of rnd.

## Shape First Crown

Note: Change to circular needle when necessary.

1st rnd: Kfb in each st around. 16 sts.

2nd rnd: *K1. Kfb. Rep from * around. 24 sts.

3rd rnd: *K2. Kfb. Rep from * around. 32 sts.

4th rnd: *K3. Kfb. Rep from * around. 40 sts.

5th rnd: *K4. Kfb. Rep from * around. 48 sts.

6th rnd: *K5. Kfb. Rep from * around. 56 sts.

7th rnd: *K6. Kfb. Rep from * around. 64 sts.

8th rnd: *K7. Kfb. Rep from * around. 72 sts.

9th rnd: (K17. Kfb) 4 times. 76 sts. PM at end of last rnd.

## Cont with Body as follows:

Work in stocking st (knit each rnd) until work from marker measures 11" [28 cm]. Cut yarn and rejoin yarn from darkest end of O'Go. Work in stocking st until work from color change measures 11" [28 cm].

## Shape Second Crown

Note: Change to double pointed needles when necessary.

1st rnd: *(K17. K2tog) 4 times. 72 sts.

2nd rnd: *K7. K2tog. Rep from * around. 64 sts.

3rd rnd: *K6. K2tog. Rep from * around. 56 sts.

4th rnd: *K5. K2tog. Rep from * around. 48 sts.

5th rnd: *K4. K2tog. Rep from * around. 40 sts.

6th rnd: *K3. K2tog. Rep from * around. 32 sts.

7th rnd: *K2. K2tog. Rep from * around. 24 sts.

8th rnd: *K1. K2tog. Rep from * around. 16 sts.

9th rnd: (K2tog) 8 times. 8 sts. Break yarn leaving a 12" [30.5 cm] long yarn tail. Draw tail tightly through rem sts and fasten securely.

## FINISHING

With yarn needle, weave tail from cast-on tightly through 8 cast-on sts and tighten to close hole. Fasten securely. Fold Hat in half by pushing Second Crown into First Crown to create double thickness (as shown in photo). Hat is fully reversible and can be worn with or without 3" [7.5 cm] folded brim.

Pretty Hats to Knit

# Caron Lumberjack Beanie

SKILL LEVEL: EASY

**MATERIALS**

Caron® Simply Soft® (6 oz/170.1 g; 315 yds/288 m)

Contrast A Harvest Red (39763) 1 ball

Contrast B Black (39727) 1 ball

Size U.S. 8 (5 mm) knitting needles or size needed to obtain gauge. Yarn needle. 11 stitch markers

## ABBREVIATIONS

Alt = Alternate

Approx = Approximately

Beg = Beginning

Cont = Continue(ity)

Dec = Decrease(ing)

K = Knit

K2tog = Knit next 2 stitches together

Pat = Pattern

Rem = Remain(ing)

Rep = Repeat

RS = Right side

Ssk = Slip next 2 stitches knitwise one at a time. Pass them back onto left-hand needle, then knit through back loops together

St(s) = Stitch(es)

WS = Wrong side

**SIZE:** One size to fit average Adult.

**GAUGE:** 17 sts and 32 rows = 4" [10 cm] in garter st.

## INSTRUCTIONS

**Stripe Pat**

With A, knit 14 rows.

With B, knit 14 rows.

These 28 rows form Stripe Pat.

Cast on 82 sts.

Proceed in Stripe Pat in garter st (knit every row) until work from beg measures 8" [20.5 cm], noting first row is RS and ending on a WS row.

Shape top: Keeping cont of Stripe Pat, dec as follows: 1st row: (RS). K1. *K2tog. ssk. K16. Rep from * to last st. K1. 74 sts.

2nd and alt rows: Knit.

3rd row: K1. *K2tog. ssk. K14. Rep from * to last st. K1. 66 sts.

5th row: K1. *K2tog. ssk. K12. Rep from * to last st. K1. 58 sts.

7th row: K1. *K2tog. ssk. K10. Rep from * to last st. K1. 50 sts.

9th row: K1. *K2tog. ssk. K8. Rep from * to last st. K1. 42 sts.

11th row: K1. *K2tog. ssk. K6. Rep from * to last st. K1. 34 sts.

13th row: K1. *K2tog. ssk. K4. Rep from * to last st. K1. 26 sts.

15th row: K1. *K2tog. ssk. K2. Rep from * to last st. K1. 18 sts.

16th row: *K2tog. Rep from * to end of row. 9 sts. Break yarn, leaving a long end.

Draw end tightly through rem sts and fasten securely.

**Vertical weaving:** Beg 1 st in from side edge, place markers on every 8th st along cast on edge of Hat, dividing Hat into 10 even sections.

Thread a long length of B through yarn needle. With RS facing and beg at bottom edge, weave yarn over and under through vertical columns of garter stitch "bumps" up to top edge and back down to the bottom edge until a column of 8 sts has been woven.

Note: Adjust weaving as needed to accommodate for fewer sts at decrease section at top of Hat.

Work 4 more columns of weaving in same manner, leaving a section of 8 unwoven sts between each section of 8 woven sts.

Sew center back seam.

# Patons Bright Stripes Beanie

**SKILL LEVEL: EASY**

# Pretty Hats to Knit

## MATERIALS

Patons® Classic Wool Roving™ (3.5 oz/100 g; 120 yds/109 m)

Contrast A Pacific Teal (77203) 1 ball

Contrast B Cherry (77709) 1 ball

Contrast C Pumpkin (77605) 1 ball

Contrast D Cloverleaf (77222) 1 ball

Size U.S. 10½ (6.5 mm) knitting needles or size needed to obtain gauge.

## ABBREVIATIONS

Alt = Alternate(ing)

Beg = Beginning

Cont = Continue(ity)

K = Knit

K2tog = Knit next 2 stitches together

P = Purl

Pat = Pattern

Rem = Remain(ing)

Rep = Repeat

RS = Right side

St(s) = Stitch(es)

WS = Wrong side

**SIZE:** One size to fit average woman's head.

**GAUGE:** 14 sts and 18 rows = 4"[10 cm] in stocking st.

## INSTRUCTIONS

With A, cast on 68 sts.

1st row: (RS). *K2. P1. Rep from * to last 2 sts. K2.

2nd row: *P2. K1. Rep from * to last 2 sts. P2.

Rep last 2 rows of (K2. P1) ribbing once more, then 1st row once.

Proceed in pat as follows:

1st row: (WS). With D, knit.

2nd row: With D, knit.

3rd and 4th rows: With C, knit.

# Pretty Hats to Knit

5th and 6th rows: With B, knit.

7th and 8th rows: With A, knit.

These 8 rows form Stripe Pat.

Cont in Stripe Pat until work from beg measures 6" [15 cm], ending on a RS row.

**Shape top**: Keeping cont of Stripe Pat, proceed as follows:

1st row: (WS). *K7. K2tog. K8. Rep from * to end of row. 64 sts.

2nd and alt rows: Knit.

3rd row: K1. (K2tog. K5) 9 times. 55 sts.

5th row: K1. (K2tog. K4) 9 times. 46 sts.

7th row: K1. (K2tog. K3) 9 times. 37 sts.

9th row: K1. (K2tog. K2) 9 times. 28 sts.

11th row: K1. (K2tog. K1) 9 times. 19 sts.

Break yarn, leaving a long end. Draw end tightly through rem sts. Sew center back seam.

**Pompom**: Wrap A, B, C and D around 3 fingers 25 times. Remove from fingers and tie tightly in center. Cut through each side of loops.

Trim to a smooth round shape. Sew securely to top of Hat.

# Red Heart Ribbed Knit Beanie

**Version 1**

**Version 2**

**MATERIALS**

Red Heart® Super Saver® O'Go™ (Prints: 5 oz/141 g; 236 yds/215 m)

**Version 1**

Forest (7136) 1 O'Go

# Pretty Hats to Knit

**Version 2**

Jeweltone (7195) 1 O'Go

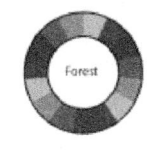

## ABBREVIATIONS

Beg = Beginning

Center dec = (worked over 3 sts) Slip next 2 stitches as if to K2tog. K1, then pass slipped sts over knit st – center of 3 stitches should be on top of decrease. 2 stitches have been decreased

K = Knit

K2tog = Knit next 2 stitches together

P = Purl

PM = Place marker

Rem = Remain(ing)

Rep = Repeat

Rnd(s) = Round(s)

Ssk = Slip next 2 stitches knitwise one at a time. Pass them back onto left-hand needle, then knit through back loops together

St(s) = Stitch(es)

**SIZE:** One size to fit adult.

**GAUGE:** 18 sts and 24 rows = 4" [10 cm] in stocking stitch.

**INSTRUCTIONS**

Notes:

• Hat is knit to a tighter-than average gauge. Please check gauge to ensure satisfactory results.

• To begin working with the O'Go format, carefully cut plastic tie where the ends of the O'Go meet.

• Pull tie to remove.

With circular needle, cast on 84 sts.

Join in rnd. PM for beg of rnd.

1st rnd: *K1. P1. Rep from * around. Rep last rnd (K1. P1) ribbing until work from beg measures 10" [25.5 cm].

**Shape top:**

# Pretty Hats to Knit

Note: Change to double-pointed needles when necessary.

1st rnd: *(K1. P1) twice. ssk. K1. K2tog. P1. K1. P1. Rep from * around. 70 sts.

2nd to 6th rnds: *(K1. P1) twice. K3. P1. K1. P1. Rep from * around.

7th rnd: *(K1. P1) twice. Center dec. P1. K1. P1. 56 sts.

8th to 12th rnds: *K1. P1. Rep from * around.

13th rnd: *K1. P1. ssk. K1. K2tog. P1. Rep from * around. 42 sts.

14th to 16th rnds: *K1. P1. K3. P1. Rep from * around.

17th rnd: *K1. P1. Center dec. P1. Rep from * around. 28 sts.

18th rnd: *K1. P1. Rep from * around.

19th rnd: *K1. Center dec. Rep from * around. 14 sts.

20th rnd: *K2tog. Rep from * around. 7 sts.

Break yarn, leaving a long end.

Draw end through rem sts and fasten securely.

# Patons Breezy Knit Beret

**SKILL LEVEL:** Easy

**MATERIALS**

Patons® Norse™ (3.5 oz/100 g; 211 yds/193 m) Camel (91005) 1 ball

Sizes U.S. 9 (5.5 mm) and U.S. 10 (6 mm) circular knitting needles 16" [40.5 cm] long. Set of 4 size U.S. 10 (6 mm) double-pointed knitting needles or size needed to obtain gauge. Stitch marker. Yarn needle.

## ABBREVIATIONS

Alt = Alternate

Beg = Begin(ning)

Cont = Continue

Dec = Decreasing

K = Knit

K2tog = Knit next 2 stitches together

Kfb = Increase 1 stitch by knitting into front and back of next stitch

P = Purl

PM = Place marker

Rep = Repeat

Rnd(s) = Round(s)

St(s) = Stitch(es)

**SIZE:** One size to fit Adult.

## GAUGE

# Pretty Hats to Knit

15 sts and 18 rows = 4" [10 cm] in stocking stitch with larger needles.

## INSTRUCTIONS

With smaller circular needle, cast on 64 sts. PM. Join to beg working in rnd.

1st rnd: *K1. P1. Rep from * around. Rep last rnd of (K1. P1) ribbing 5 times more.

Change to larger circular needle and proceed as follows:

1st and alt rnds: Knit.

2nd rnd: *K7. Kfb. Rep from * around. 72 sts.

4th rnd: *K8. Kfb. Rep from * around. 80 sts.

6th rnd: *K9. Kfb. Rep from * around. 88 sts.

8th rnd: *K10. Kfb. Rep from * around. 96 sts.

10th rnd: *K11. Kfb. Rep from * around. 104 sts.

12th rnd: *K12. Kfb. Rep from * around. 112 sts.

Knit 12 rnds even.

***Shape top:*** 1st rnd: *K12. K2tog. Rep from * around. 104 sts.

2nd rnd: *K11. K2tog. Rep from * around. 96 sts.

3rd rnd: *K10. K2tog. Rep from * around. 88 sts.

4th rnd: *K9. K2tog. Rep from * around. 80 sts.

5th rnd: *K8. K2tog. Rep from * around. 72 sts.

6th rnd: *K7. K2tog. Rep from * around. 64 sts.

7th rnd: *K6. K2tog. Rep from * around. 56 sts.

Cont as established, dec 8 sts every rnd until there are 16 sts, changing to double-pointed needles when appropriate.

Next rnd: (K2tog) 8 times. 8 sts.

Next rnd: (K2tog) 4 times. 4 sts.

### *I-cord Stem*

Slip all 4 sts onto one doublepointed needle. Do not turn.

1st row: *Slide sts to other end of needle. K4. Do not turn.

Rep last row 3 times more.

Next row: (K2tog) twice.

Next row: K2tog. Fasten off.

Pretty Hats to Knit

# Red Heart Buttoned Beret

**SKILL LEVEL:** Intermediate

**MATERIALS:**

STITCH NATION by Debbie Stoller™ "Full o' Sheep™":

# Pretty Hats to Knit

1 ball 2550 Plummy.

Circular Knitting Needles: 4.5mm [US 7] 16".

Double Pointed Needles: One set 4.5mm [US 7].

Place markers (8), 2 buttons 1" diameter, yarn needle.

**ABBREVIATIONS**

Inc = increase;

k = knit;

p = purl;

st[s] = stitch[es];

tog = together;

yo = yarn over needle;

* or ** = repeat whatever follows the * or ** as indicated.

Ssk = Slip 2 sts knitwise one at a time to right needle, insert point of left needle into front of sts, and knit them together.

**SIZE:** One size fits most. Hat circumference: 21"

**GAUGE:** 17 sts = 4"; 29 rounds = 4" in Seed stitch.

# Pretty Hats to Knit

## Notes

After working cuff, hat is worked in the round. As stitches are decreased and no longer fit on circular needles, divide them among 3 double pointed needles to complete.

K1, p1 Rib (over an odd number of sts)

Row 1 (Right Side): K1, * p1, k1; repeat from * across.

Row 2: P1,* k1, p1; repeat from * across.

Repeat Rows 1 and 2 for K1, p1 rib.

*Seed Stitch* (over an even number of sts)

Round 1: * K1, p1; repeat from around.

Round 2: * P1, k1; repeat from * around (that is, p the knit sts and k the purl sts).

## BERET

With circular needles, cast on 87 sts. Do not join, but work back and forth in rows.

### Brim

Begin with Row 1, work 3 rows in K1, p1 rib.

Buttonhole Row (Wrong Side): Rib 3, yo, p2tog, rib to end of row.

Continue in rib for 3 rows.

Next Row (Wrong Side): Bind off first 7 sts for tab, rib to end of row–80 sts.

### *Setup Pattern*

Next Row: * Inc by knitting into front and back of next st, [p1, k1] 4 times, inc by purling into front and back of next st, place marker; repeat from * across, omitting last marker–96 sts.

### *Join*

Place marker for beginning of round and join to complete Beret as follows:

Next Round: * K1, p1; repeat from * around.

Next Round: * Inc by purling into front and back of next st, [k1, p1] 5 times, inc by knitting into front and back of next st; repeat from * around–112 sts.

Keeping continuity of pattern, work even in Seed st until piece measures 4" from joining, end with Round 1.

### *Setup Crown Pattern and Shaping*

Round 1: * [P1, k1] 2 times, p1, k2tog, p1, k1, [k1, p1] 2 times, k1; repeat from * around–104 sts.

Round 2: * [K1, p1] 2 times, k2, [p1, k1] 3 times, p1, repeat from * around.

Round 3: * [P1, k1] 4 times, k1, [p1, k1] 2 times; repeat from * around.

Round 4: * K1, p1, k1, P2tog, k1, p1, k1, k2tog, p1, k1, p1; repeat from * around–88 sts.

Round 5: * [P1, k1] 2 times, [k1, p1] 3 times, k1; repeat from * around.

Round 6: * [K1, p1] 3 times, k1, [k1, p1] 2 times; repeat from * around.

Round 7: * P1, k1, p2tog, k1, p1, k1, k2tog, p1, k1; repeat from * around–72 sts.

Round 8: * K1, p1, k2, [p1, k1] 2 times, p1; repeat from * around.

Round 9: * [P1, k1] 3 times, k1, p1, k1; repeat from * around.

Round 10: * K1, p1, k1, ssk, k1, k2tog, p1; repeat from * around–56 sts.

Round 11: * P1, k1, p1, k2, p1, k1; repeat from * around.

Round 12: * K1, p1, k4, p1; repeat from * around.

Round 13: * P1, ssk, k2, k2tog; repeat from * around–40 sts.

Round 14: * K1, p1, k2, p1; repeat from * around.

Round 15: * P1, k4; repeat from * around.

Round 16: * K1, k3tog, p1; repeat from * around–24 sts.

Round 17: * P1, k2; repeat from * around.

Round 18: * K3tog; repeat from * around–8 sts.

Cut yarn leaving a long tail. Thread tail through remaining sts and pull tightly to secure.

## FINISHING

Overlap tab 1" and mark placement on cuff for first button opposite buttonhole. Mark placement for second button on cuff 1" to the left of first button (no buttonhole). Sew buttons to cuff. Weave in yarn ends.

Pretty Hats to Knit

# Red Heart Cabled Chapeau

**SKILL LEVEL:** Easy

**MATERIALS:**

STITCH NATION by Debbie Stoller™ "Alpaca Love™": 2 balls

# Pretty Hats to Knit

3520 Peacock Feather.

Circular Knitting Needles: 5 mm [US 8] 16".

Knitting Needles: 5 mm [US 8] straight.

1 Set Double-Pointed Needles: 5 mm [US 8].

Cable needle, stitch markers, yarn needle, sewing thread and needle, 2 buttons 1" diameter, empty whipped topping container or other round piece of plastic for brim.

## ABBREVIATIONS:

dec = decrease;

k = knit;

p = purl;

st(s) = stitch(es);

tog = together;

[ ] = work directions in brackets the number of times specified; * or ** = repeat whatever follows the * or ** as indicated

4/4 LPC: Slip next 4 sts to cable needle and hold to front, k4, k4 from cable needle.

### *Cable Pattern Stitch (multiple of 12 sts)*

Rounds 1-7: * K8, p4; repeat from * around.

Round 8: * 4/4 LPC, p4; repeat from * around.

Rounds 9 and 10: * K8, p4; repeat from * around.

Repeat Rounds 1 - 10 for stitch pattern.

**SIZE:** Hat circumference is 22". One size fits most women

**GAUGE:** 18 sts = 4"; 24 rows = 4" in pattern stitch.

## NOTES

Hat is worked in the round. As stitches are decreased and no longer fit on circular needles, divide them among 3 double pointed needles to complete.

## HAT

With circular needles, cast on 96 sts. Place marker for beginning of round and join, being careful not to twist sts.

### *Cuff Ribbing*

Round 1: * K1, p1; repeat from * around.

Repeat Round 1 twice more.

Next Round: Begin Cable Stitch Pattern. Work until hat measures 7" from beginning.

## *Shape Crown*

Round 1 (dec): * [K2 tog] 4 times, [p2tog] 2 times; repeat from * around–48 sts.

Rounds 2 and 3: * K4, p2; repeat from * around.

Round 4 (dec): * [K2tog] 2 times, p2 tog; repeat from * around–24 sts.

Round 5: * K2, p1; repeat from * around.

Round 6: * K2tog, p1: repeat from * around–16 sts.

## *Finishing*

Cut yarn leaving long tail. Thread yarn through remaining sts to secure. Weave in yarn ends.

## *Brim*

With knitting needles, cast on 40 sts. Begin with a right side row, work in St st and work short-row shaping as follows:

Row 1: Knit 25, turn.

Row 2: Slip 1, p12; turn.

Row 3: Slip 1, k15; turn.

Row 4: Slip 1, p18; turn.

Continue to work in this manner, working 3 more sts at center each time until all 40 sts have been worked. Work 6 rows even in St st. Bind off 2 sts at beginning of next 10 rows–20 sts. Bind off 3 sts at the beginning of next 4 rows–8 sts. Bind off.

## *Strap*

With knitting needles, cast on 7 sts.

Row 1: K1, *p1, k1; repeat from * across.

Row 2: P1, *k1, p1; repeat from * across.

Repeat Rows 1 and 2 until strap measures 8". Bind off in pattern.

Weave in ends.

## **FINISHING**

Fold brim in half with knit side to the outside. Cut plastic to the shape of the brim. Slip plastic inside brim and sew edges together. Sew brim to center front of cap. Pin strap above brim as shown and sew to cap while sewing on buttons. Weave in ends.